Ghana

Camilla de la Bédoyère

WAYLAND

First published in 2011 by Wayland
Copyright Wayland 2011

Wayland
Hachette Children's Books
338 Euston Road
London NW1 3BH

Wayland Australia
Level 17/207 Kent Street,
Sydney, NSW 2000

Concept design: Jason Billin
Editors: Nicola Edwards and Kelly Davis
Designer: Amy Sparks
Consultants: Yaw Appiah and Elaine Jackson

Produced for Wayland by
White-Thomson Publishing Ltd

www.wtpub.co.uk
+44 (0) 0843 2087 460

British Library Cataloguing in Publication Data

De la Bédoyère, Camilla
Ghana -- (Discover countries)
1. Ghana -- Juvenile literature
I. Title II. Series 966.7'053-dc22

ISBN-13: 978 0750 2 6450 1

Printed in Malaysia
Wayland is a division of Hachette Children's Books
an Hachette UK company
www.hachette.co.uk

All data in this book was researched in 2010
and has been collected from the latest sources available at that time.

Contents

Discovering Ghana

Ghana is a young, developing nation in West Africa, known for its natural beauty and blend of cultures. It is about the size of the United Kingdom, but with less than half the UK's population. Ghana is close to the Equator so it has a very hot climate. Its economy is strong, compared to other West African nations, but many of its people still live in poverty. Ghana has a democratic government, led by a president.

Ghana statistics

Area: 238,533 sq km (92,098 sq miles)

Capital city: Accra

Government type: Constitutional democracy

Bordering countries: Burkina Faso, Ivory Coast, Togo

Currency: Ghana cedi (GHc)

Language: Asante 14.8%, Ewe 12.7%, Fante 9.9%, Boron (Brong) 4.6%, Dagomba 4.3%, Dangme 4.3%, Dagarte (Dagaba) 3.7%, Akyem 3.4%, Ga 3.4%, Akuapem 2.9%, other 36.1% (includes English (official))

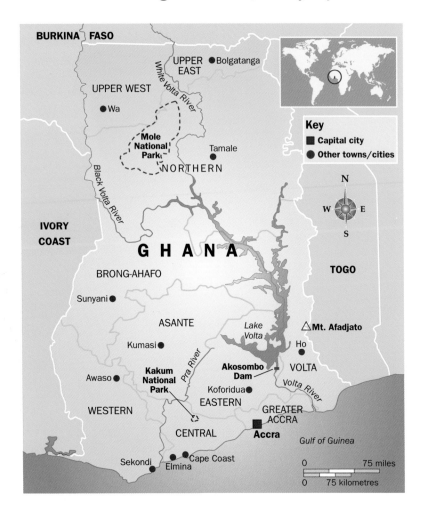

A map of Ghana showing the ten administrative regions: Upper West, Upper East, Northern, Brong-Ahafo, Asante, Western, Central, Eastern, Greater Accra, and Volta.

A young nation

Ghana has a rich and complex history. In the seventeenth century, the Asante (or Ashanti) Empire rose to power in the region, conquering neighbouring states. The region became known as the Gold Coast when Europeans came in search of precious minerals, and to trade goods such as guns and cloth in exchange for gold and humans.

Slavery already existed, but it became big business, especially for the Portuguese and the British, causing untold misery for the people who were enslaved and the families left behind.

The country was a British colony from 1874 until 1957, when Ghana (as it was named) became the first African nation to gain independence. English is still the official language of Ghana, although other languages, such as Asante, Ga and Ewe, are spoken.

Land of Gold

This region was once known as the Land of Gold, or the Gold Coast, because it is rich in resources, such as gold and cacao (which is used to make chocolate) and fertile enough, in many places, for farmers to grow crops. Because of Ghana's natural wealth, and its position on the Gulf of Guinea, these African shores have a long history of international trade, and settlers from other parts of Africa and Europe have made their homes here.

DID YOU KNOW?
The red band of Ghana's flag represents the blood of those who fought for independence, the yellow represents gold and the green represents forests. A black star symbolises freedom.

For hundreds of years, traders have sailed to Ghana's coastline to conduct their business.

Landscape and climate

Ghana is a country of two halves. Its northern region is hot and dry but in the southern region there are large areas of lush, tropical rainforest. The land in Ghana is mostly low-lying, apart from a range of hills at its eastern border with Togo.

Sun and seasons

Thanks to its position close to the Equator, Ghana does not have seasons such as winter and summer. The climate is hot all year round. But while the southern areas are often humid and enjoy two rainy seasons a year, some places in the northern plains and central region have just one short rainy season.

Facts at a glance

Water area: 11,000 sq km (4,247 miles)

Highest point: Mount Afadjato 880 m (2,887 ft)

Lowest point: Atlantic Ocean 0 m (0 ft)

Longest river: Volta River 1,600 km (1,000 miles)

Coastline: 539 km (335 miles)

The harmattan winds sweep sand across Ghana's landscape. The sand can cause damage to people's lungs, but it also helps control disease-bearing mosquitoes.

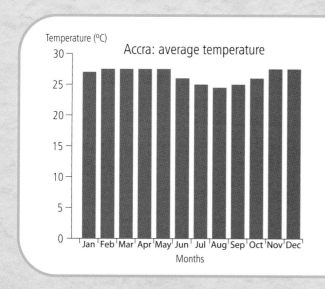

Temperature (°C)

Accra: average temperature

Months

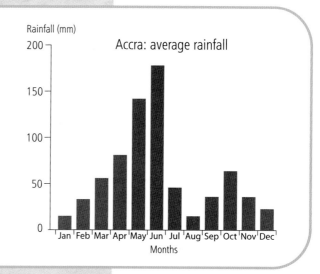

Rainfall (mm)

Accra: average rainfall

Months

Deserts, savannah and forests

The hot, dry conditions in northern Ghana occasionally cause droughts (long periods with no rainfall) that bring great hardship to the people living there. Around 35 per cent of Ghana's land is vulnerable to desertification – during this process fertile land (including farmland) that could once support plant life gradually becomes desert. Areas further south that receive more rainfall can support large grasslands, called savannahs, and in the wettest places tropical rainforests thrive.

Lake Volta

Lake Volta is 400 km (250 miles) long and one of the largest artificial lakes in the world. It was created in the 1960s when the Akosombo Dam was built to hold back the River Volta as it flowed towards the Gulf of Guinea. The creation of this enormous reservoir of water resulted in the flooding of 15,000 homes, and 78,000 people had to be resettled. However, water from the lake is now used to generate power and to irrigate farms.

▼ This boy is one of thousands employed in the fishing industry around Lake Volta.

Population and health

Like most other African nations, Ghana is home to people from different ethnic groups, or tribes. Ghanaian groups include the Akan, Ewe, Mole-Dagbon, Ga-Dangme and Gurma. They have their own languages, traditions and cultures but most tribes live peacefully side by side.

Ethnic groups

Nearly half of all Ghanaians are from the Akan ethnic group, which includes speakers of many languages, including Asante and Fante. Most Akan people live in the south and west of the country. Their family groups, or clans, are led by women. Most Ewe people live in the south-east of the country and their large family groups are normally led by male chiefs.

Facts at a glance

Total population:
23.8 million

Life expectancy at birth:
61 years

Children dying before the age of five: 7.6%

Ethnic composition: Akan 45%, Mole-Dagbon 15%, Ewe 12%, Ga-Dangme 7%, Guan 4%, Gurma 4%, Grusi 3%, Other tribes, including Dagomba 2%, other 8%

▶ Most rural people do not have access to piped water. Children collect water from rivers or wells, and carry it home. They may spend several hours a day carrying out this chore.

A growing population

The population of Ghana has been steadily growing in recent times, and advances in medical care mean it is likely to stay high for some time to come. Fewer babies and young children are dying, and life expectancy in Ghana is one of the longest in West Africa.

Health problems

In general, Ghanaians enjoy better health than many of their neighbours in West Africa, but they still face many of the problems that affect people in the developing world. Conditions such as malaria, diarrhoea and lung infections are common causes of death in children and babies. Adults are more likely to suffer from HIV infection and diabetes, or be killed in road traffic accidents. Malnutrition, caused by a diet with too few calories and nutrients, is a major cause of ill-health for people living in the poorest areas. The Ghanaian government is working hard to solve these problems, with assistance from the World Health Organization.

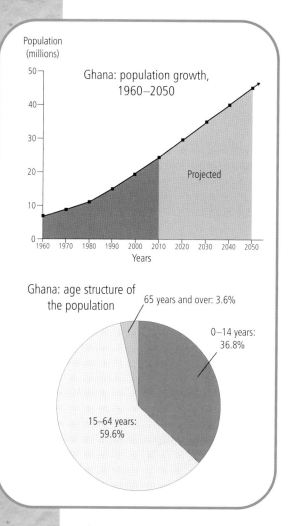

Population (millions)

Ghana: population growth, 1960–2050

Projected

Years

Ghana: age structure of the population

65 years and over: 3.6%

0–14 years: 36.8%

15–64 years: 59.6%

◀ Community Health Nurses treat illnesses, vaccinate children and provide health advice at this child welfare clinic in Koforidua.

Settlements and living

In 1960, about a quarter of Ghana's population lived in towns. Since then, the trend towards urban (town) life has grown rapidly, and it is predicted that by 2020 more than half of the population will live in towns, rather than in rural (countryside) areas.

Accra

Ghana's capital city is Accra and it is estimated that about 2 million people now live in the city and another 2 million around it. The government and administrative offices are based in Accra, and it is a busy, thriving city. Urban populations in Accra and other cities have swelled in recent years, because many people move to the city in search of work. Those who succeed in finding good jobs live in apartment blocks or smart homes in the wealthiest parts of the city.

Facts at a glance

Urban population: 50% (12 million)

Rural population: 50% (11.7 million)

Population of largest city: 2.1 million (Accra)

▼ The town of Elmina is on Ghana's coast. The style of building is influenced by a long history of European visitors and immigrants.

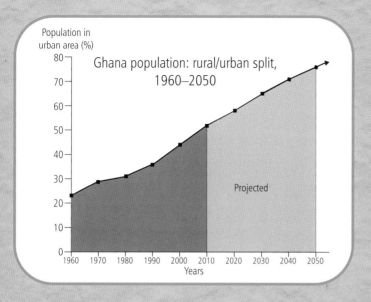

Population in urban area (%)

Ghana population: rural/urban split, 1960–2050

Projected

Years

Rural homes

In rural areas, the homes are often made from mud called adobe, which dries hard in the hot Ghanaian sunshine. In northern regions, the women build their homes, and decorate them with bold patterns and colours. Houses are often grouped in small settlements and the people who live there work in the fields and farms.

A hard life

Rural life can be very tough, and nearly half the people in rural areas live below the poverty line. This means they do not always have enough to eat, and rural children are less likely to survive into adulthood than urban children. Rural families spend much of their time collecting firewood and water, and tending their crops and animals.

The Kusasi people of north-eastern Ghana build round houses from clay. The roofs are thatched with grass, which is lightweight and reasonably waterproof. Entrances are small to keep the inside of the houses cool.

DID YOU KNOW? It is estimated that more than 5 million Ghanaians (around one-fifth of the total population) live in urban slums, where they build makeshift houses, without proper access to clean water, education or healthcare.

Family life

Ghanaians believe families and children are gifts to be treasured. Families are large, and include not only parents and their children but grandparents, aunts, uncles and cousins, who all share the care of youngsters and elderly relatives.

United by marriage

The tradition of marriage is strong in Ghana, but attitudes are changing. More unmarried couples now live together than before, and divorce is also more common. Women usually marry in their early twenties, and are expected to start their families soon after marriage. On average, women have around four children. About one-third of all marriages in northern Ghana are polygamous, which means a man has more than one wife.

Facts at a glance

Average children per childbearing woman:
3.6 children

Average household size:
4 people

▶ Girls wear Bodom beads during coming-of-age ceremonies. The beads are made of powdered glass and are very valuable. They are handed down through generations.

Welcome to the world

When a baby is born the family comes together to celebrate. Naming ceremonies are also popular because a Ghanaian's name is regarded as one of the most important things they can own. Depending on their tribal customs, a Ghanaian child might be given a family name, a tribal name, a birthday name and a nickname, as well as religious or 'praise names'.

A time for celebration

Funerals in Ghana are lengthy, stylish and often expensive events. The whole family attends a funeral, which is often seen as a celebration, and a reason to rejoice, as their loved one moves on to a better world. Red and black clothing is traditional at funerals, but fantasy coffins are a more modern custom. These hand-built caskets reflect the life of the person who has died – and may be in the shape of cars, mobile phones or even sharks!

DID YOU KNOW?
When an Akan baby is eight days old it is given a naming ceremony. The baby is named after the day of the week when it was born. So a boy named Yaw would have been born on Thursday.

A brightly painted fish coffin is carefully carried across an Accra street by the carpenters who made it.

Religion and beliefs

Ghanaians are religious people who are allowed to practise their faiths in freedom. People of different faiths live side by side, and the nation is known for its religious tolerance. Christianity and Islam are the two largest world faiths found in Ghana, but traditional beliefs are also practised throughout the country.

Christianity in Ghana

Portuguese travellers first brought Christianity to the country more than 500 years ago, but this religion did not take hold until missionaries re-introduced it in the nineteenth century. Most Christians belong to Catholic or Protestant Churches.

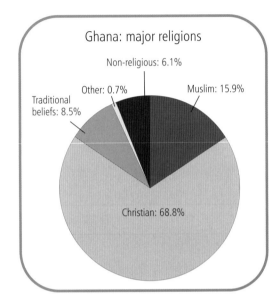

Ghana: major religions

Non-religious: 6.1%

Other: 0.7%

Traditional beliefs: 8.5%

Muslim: 15.9%

Christian: 68.8%

▼ During the festival of Palm Sunday, processions of Christians pray and carry palm leaves. The day marks the beginning of Holy Week, which ends on Easter Sunday.

Islam in Ghana

In the north of Ghana, Islam is the most widely practised world faith. Traders from North Africa introduced Islam to Ghana as long ago as the eighth century. Nigerian Muslims, who fled to Ghana in order to escape persecution in the nineteenth century, have also added to the numbers of those following Islam.

Traditional religions

Ghanaians are so tolerant of different religions that many of them are able to combine Christian or Muslim faiths with the traditional beliefs of their ancestors. Traditional religions are based on the idea of a single supreme god, and lesser gods who are connected to the natural world and spirits. Ancestors are believed to become part of the spirit world, and watch over their families.

Some Ghanaians practise Voodoo, a traditional African religion. Followers of Voodoo combine magical and spiritual rituals, such as animal sacrifices, music and dancing, spells and worshipping their ancestors.

⬭ There are many examples of Islamic architecture in northern Ghana. Here, an imam (Muslim religious leader) and two young Muslims stand outside a thirteenth-century mosque.

DID YOU KNOW?
Ghanaians often share their faith by giving their businesses religious names, such as 'God is Good Taxis' or decorating them with slogans, such as 'Remember Now Thy Creator'.

Education and learning

Ghanaians and their government value education, and all children are offered a free education until they reach senior secondary school – normally around the age of 12. Although the government has recently spent a lot of money on improving the education system, some children are still unable to go to school.

Barriers to learning

Children are expected to attend primary school for six years, and junior secondary school for another three. An equal number of boys and girls go to primary school, but nearly 30 per cent of Ghanaian children do not get an education.

Facts at a glance

Children in primary school:
Male 73%, Female 71%

Children in secondary school:
Male 47%, Female 43%

Literacy rate (over 15 years):
58%

A young girl works hard at her schoolwork. Ghanaian children regard education as a privilege, not a chore.

Their families may not be able to afford the cost of uniforms and books, or they may live too far from a school. The families of children who want to attend senior secondary school have to pay for their education.

Lessons and languages

When children start primary school they are taught in their local Ghanaian language, but as they get older they are taught in English, which is the language of business in Ghana. Like children all over the world, they learn reading, writing and arithmetic. Sports, arts and crafts, and agriculture are also part of the curriculum.

The brain drain

When they have completed their secondary school education, students may apply for a place at a university or polytechnic. Once qualified, many students choose to take their skills and knowledge and work abroad. More than 50 per cent of doctors trained in Ghana now work in other countries, seeking a better life. This migration, or 'brain drain', has caused problems in Ghana, and a shortage of skilled staff in schools, universities and hospitals.

DID YOU KNOW?
Ghanaian children from rural areas are less likely to be able to read than those from urban areas, and fewer than 10 per cent of people in northern rural areas learn how to read and write.

▶ Students at an international school in Accra learn how to construct sentences in English.

Employment and economy

Compared to many African countries, Ghana has a stable economy that has been steadily growing for more than 20 years. Most of the country's wealth is created in the southern region. However, up to one-third of all Ghanaians still live in poverty, which means they are unlikely to be educated, or have jobs or access to healthcare.

Rich in resources

Although Ghana has been through some difficult economic times, it has good natural resources that it can use to keep building a stronger, wealthier future. Ghana has valuable minerals, such as gold and diamonds, and its rich, fertile land supports about half of the population, who work in agriculture.

Facts at a glance

Contributions to GDP:
 agriculture: 37%
 industry: 25%
 services: 38%
Labour force:
 agriculture: 56%
 industry: 15%
 services: 29%
Female labour force:
 49% of total
Unemployment rate: 11%

▶ Kente cloth is a famous Ghanaian product, which provides employment for both men and women. It is woven on traditional looms by men or boys. Women then stitch the strips of cloth together, and sell it.

> ▶ Colourful pots on sale in a town near Accra. Pottery-making is mainly done by women, often on a small scale.

Working women

Despite having to care for their families, 87 per cent of Ghanaian women work as well. Their labour is often unpaid (such as working their land) or poorly paid. Women are more likely to be self-employed than men, running their own small businesses, and therefore do not benefit from job security or a steady wage.

Working to cut poverty

In the year 2000 the Ghanaian government committed itself to a Millennium Development Goal. Their plan is to cut poverty by half by 2015 and they expect to do this by helping businesses make more profit, improving agriculture and developing rural communities. However, natural events such as droughts, severe rains and flooding, and problems with the electricity supply, can cause sudden emergencies and damage the economy. Foreign countries give money – aid – to Ghana to support its efforts to cut poverty. For example, in 2009 the UK gave Ghana £100 million and the US gave $148 million.

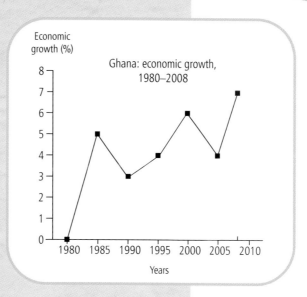

Economic growth (%)

Ghana: economic growth, 1980–2008

Years

Industry and trade

Ghana's industry provides one-third of the country's gross domestic product (GDP) but Ghana buys more goods from abroad than it sells. Ghana trades with many countries, including Nigeria, China, the US, the UK, Germany and Togo.

Mining for wealth

Centuries ago, people travelled to West Africa because of its rich mineral

resources. Today those resources, such as gold and diamonds, still bring wealth and work to the region. Ghana is one of the world's leading producers of gold, which is mined. Bauxite is also mined: this mineral is smelted at a factory powered by the Akosombo Dam and turned into aluminium, a light but tough material used to make vehicles and in packaging and electronics.

Adding value

Ghana has an active manufacturing industry: raw materials, such as aluminium or agricultural crops, are processed to create new products that are sold around the world. Shea nuts, for example, are processed to make shea butter, which is exported for use in skin creams. The manufacturing industry helps Ghana to make more money from its exports, as well as providing jobs.

⬥ Workers at an Asante gold mine beat the soft, molten metal into blocks so it can be transported and sold.

DID YOU KNOW?
Ghana is the second-largest producer of gold in Africa, after South Africa. More than 80,000 kg (176,370 lb) of gold were mined here in 2008, yet Ghana still only produced 3.5 per cent of the world's gold for that year.

Energy to grow

Industry requires energy to make and operate machines and to fuel the transport systems that bring raw materials into factories, and take finished goods away. Electricity from the hydroelectric dam at Akosombo provides about 7 per cent of Ghana's energy needs, while firewood provides around 80 per cent.

Fuelling the future

The country will need more efficient energy sources in the future. The discovery of oilfields off Ghana's coast is expected to help reduce Ghana's energy problems. Like other African countries, Ghana is also developing cleaner, cheaper systems that use energy from the sun and wind to produce electricity, especially in rural areas.

△ The construction of the Akosombo Dam began in 1961, and it was completed in 1965.

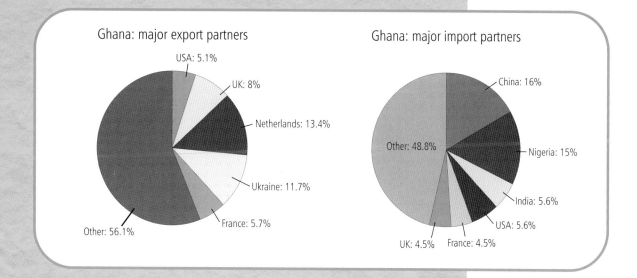

Ghana: major export partners

- USA: 5.1%
- UK: 8%
- Netherlands: 13.4%
- Ukraine: 11.7%
- France: 5.7%
- Other: 56.1%

Ghana: major import partners

- China: 16%
- Nigeria: 15%
- India: 5.6%
- USA: 5.6%
- France: 4.5%
- UK: 4.5%
- Other: 48.8%

Farming and food

More than half of all Ghanaians work in agriculture – whether they are tending their own small farms, or are employed on larger ones. Agriculture plays a major part in Ghana's economy and is responsible for about one-third of its GDP.

Growing cash crops

Cash crops are those that are grown for sale, rather than to be used by the grower. The single most important cash crop is cacao. About one-third of all the products that Ghana sells abroad come from this crop, which is turned into cocoa paste and used to make chocolate.

▼ Once the cacao beans have been removed from a pod, they can be dried and turned into cacao paste.

Ghana and its neighbour, the Ivory Coast, produce more than half of all the world's cocoa. Most cacao farmers own small plots of land, although there are some large plantations too. Other important crops include coconuts, coffee, tea and pineapples.

Forests and fisheries

For centuries, Ghana's forests and fisheries have been an important source of work and food. Logging companies cut down trees so their wood can be used in the paper and furniture industries. Fish from Lake Volta and the Gulf of Guinea feed Ghanaian families, or are sold abroad. However, both these industries have been in decline in recent years because too many trees have been cut down, and too many fish have been caught.

Subsistence farming

Most Ghanaians who work the land are subsistence farmers, particularly in the northern region. Subsistence farmers are unable to grow enough food, or raise enough livestock, to sell – they have just enough for their own families to use. In times of drought, or just before the harvest is ready, these families may go hungry and suffer from malnutrition. Common crops include cassava, yams, plantains, corn and rice, which are often used to make thick soups.

▼ Subsistence farmers spend most of their time growing and preparing food for their own families. If they produce more than they need, the extra food can be sold at the local market.

DID YOU KNOW?
Fufu, a very popular dish, is made by boiling a starchy food, such as cassava, yam or plantain, before mashing it into a thick paste. Fufu is served with a soup for added flavour.

Transport and communications

Ghanaian transport systems are a mixture of the old and the new. Roads and railways, which date from when Ghana was a British colony in the last century, are being updated because the government recognises that good transport links are essential for the economy to grow.

By road

Roads are the most important part of Ghana's transport system, especially in the southern and central regions. However, fewer than 3 in every 100 households have a car – and most of those are in or around Accra. Bicycles are more affordable, and popular: about 60 per cent of all households have one. Most of Ghana's roads are unpaved, which means the mud surfaces can become damaged and unusable during the rainy season, although aid from foreign countries has been used to improve the country's road network.

Facts at a glance

Total roads: 62,221 km (38,662 miles)

Paved roads: 9,955 km (6,186 miles)

Major airports: 2

Major ports: 1

▶ Vehicles and pedestrians jostle for space on a crowded street in Accra.

By rail

Railways were first introduced to Ghana more than a hundred years ago, to link major towns and ports. Trains are most commonly used to transport freight, such as wood, gold and bauxite, rather than people.

Keeping in touch

Modern telecommunication systems can help businesses to succeed. Mobile phones have proved to be extremely popular in Africa because landlines, for ordinary phones, are expensive to install and often unreliable. There are now more than 15 million users of mobile phones in Ghana, and that number is expected to rise. Use of the Internet, however, still lags far behind because relatively few Ghanaians can afford computers or broadband access. Only 1 per cent of Ghanaians have broadband, although Internet cafes are popular. The Ghanaian government is working to improve access to the Internet, especially in rural areas.

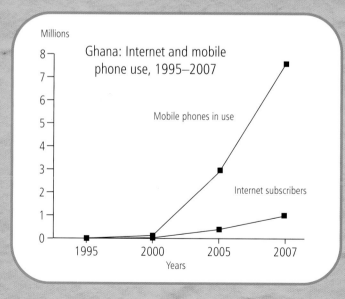

Millions

Ghana: Internet and mobile phone use, 1995–2007

Mobile phones in use

Internet subscribers

Years

DID YOU KNOW?
Tro tros are a popular form of transport in Ghana. These brightly decorated vans operate like buses and can carry up to 20 people at a time – though they are often squashed in!

🔺 Mobile phones were first used in Ghana in the early 1990s. They quickly became very popular, especially among young people.

Leisure and tourism

Football, music and dance are some of Ghana's national passions. Ghanaians enjoy many festivals throughout the year, which still resonate with the sound of traditional drum music and celebratory dances. This historic, and exciting, culture is just one of the many reasons that tourists come to Ghana.

Facts at a glance

Tourist arrivals

2000	280,000
2005	400,000
2006	430,000
2007	590,000

Musical stories

Music and dance are not just enjoyable pastimes for Ghanaians; they are used to tell stories and give news. Drums and rattles, made from gourds, are the traditional dance instruments but in recent times brass instruments, and swing and jazz elements, have been added to the ancient rhythms to create a new type of Ghanaian music, called Highlife.

▽ Elmina Castle, built by Portugese settlers in 1482, is the oldest European building south of the Sahara. Today it is a historic site visited by many tourists, especially those who are researching the history of their enslaved ancestors.

DID YOU KNOW?
Elmina Castle became an important stop in the Atlantic slave trade, which saw millions of Africans transported to work in the Americas.

The beautiful game

Ghanaians love football, and were proud and excited when their national team, the Black Stars (named after the country's flag), made it to the World Cup in 2006 and 2010. Football fans enjoy playing the game and also follow the fortunes of foreign teams, especially in the English league. Other hobbies include ludo, and playing cards, draughts and a traditional board game called oware, which is similar to backgammon.

Akwaaba!

Tourists come to Ghana to enjoy the beaches, the culture, the festivals and the wildlife and are greeted by Ghanaians with the expression 'Akwaaba', or 'welcome'. Some visitors also come to find out more about the country's rich history and their own roots – where their ancestors came from, before being sold into slavery and sent abroad.

▼ Ghanaians follow the international football scene, and youngsters practise their soccer skills in their spare time.

Environment and wildlife

Ghana's environment has provided natural resources, fertile land and rich mineral wealth, which have supported its agriculture and economy. Ghana's future success will partly depend on protecting the environment, and its government is working hard to achieve this aim.

Losing Ghana's forests

Timber was once a very important part of Ghana's wealth and economy, but deforestation is an increasing problem. It is estimated that three-quarters of Ghana's rainforests have been cut down, and some species of tree, such as mahogany, have almost disappeared. Once rainforests are destroyed they rarely come back, and the soil becomes infertile, or washes away in heavy rains. The government has set aside 15 per cent of its forest land to become nature reserves. The aim is to reduce the damage being caused to Ghana's forests, and preserve the wildlife there.

▶ In thick rainforest, a rope walkway – high above the ground – is the easiest way to get around.

Digging and dirt

Quarrying, to dig minerals from the ground, and mining can destroy the environment and affect local wildlife. Both of these processes, and the industries associated with them, pollute the soil and water. Other industries, such as clothing manufacture and brewing (to make beer), may also put dangerous chemicals into the environment.

Nature's gift

Many types of animals and plants live in Ghana, especially near the coast, in its tropical rainforests and on the savannah plains. Tourists come to Ghana to go on safari, when they can watch animals such as elephants, crocodiles and monkeys in their natural environments. Ghana's Wildlife Division has established some areas, such as the Kakum National Park, where animals and their habitats are protected. Ecotourism is being encouraged, and Ghanaians are training in wildlife management and environmental issues.

Facts at a glance

Proportion of area protected:
15%

Biodiversity (known species):
4,407

Threatened species: 139

DID YOU KNOW?
One of Ghana's most incredible animals is the Giant African snail, which grows up to 27 cm (11 inches) long. These enormous molluscs devour crops, but some people find they make a tasty, meaty treat!

The kob, seen here in Mole National Park, is the most common type of large antelope in Ghana.

Glossary

ancestor member of your family from whom you are descended

bauxite rock, or ore, that contains aluminium

colony country controlled by another country

culture way of life and traditions of a particular group of people

dam structure built to hold back, and control, a river

democratic describes a country that supports democracy, a political system where people vote for their government representatives

economy way in which trade and money are controlled by a country

Equator imaginary line drawn around the Earth, an equal distance from both Poles

ethnic describes a group of people within the population that shares a particular cultural tradition

export good or service that is sold to another country

fertile describes land or soil that can support the growth of crops

freight goods that are transported by truck, train, ship or aircraft

GDP total value of goods and services produced by a country

gourd large fruit with a hard skin

Highlife style of West African dance music that has rock and jazz elements

humid air containing a high level of water vapour

hydroelectric describes electricity generated using the power of fast-moving or falling water (water power)

import good or service that is bought from another country

independence free from control by another country or region

irrigate supply water to land to help crops to grow

life expectancy average period that a person may be expected to live

malnutrition lack of proper nutrition, caused by not having enough food or not eating enough food of the right types to give good health

manufacturing making products, usually from raw materials

mineral solid substance such as gold found in rocks or the ground

missionaries people who travel to other countries to preach religious beliefs

persecution bad treatment of someone because of their religious or political beliefs

polygamous describes the practice of having more than one wife

poverty line minimum amount of money someone needs to pay for their basic needs, such as food and shelter

rainforest forest in warm tropical regions that receives heavy rainfall all year

raw material basic material, such as cotton or gold, that can be used to make products, such as clothes or jewellery

reservoir large lake used to store water

sacrifice when an animal is killed and offered to God or to another spiritual being

slavery practice of buying and selling human beings, and keeping them to do work

subsistence farmer person who can grow just enough food for themselves and their family to eat

Topic web

**Use this topic web to explore Ghanaian themes
in different areas of your curriculum.**

History
Explore the subject of slavery. Find out how slavery affected other West African nations, and how slavery came to an end in the United States.

Science
Ghana has already lost many of its forests. What problems might deforestation cause for the region's biodiversity – the range of animals and plants that live there? Can you think of any solutions to the problem of deforestation?

Geography
Find out the names of the capital cities of Ghana's three neighbours, and learn how to spell them.

ICT
Use the Internet to find some Ghanaian recipes and find out more about the main ingredients used in Ghanaian cooking, especially yams, plantains, cassava and okra.

Ghana

Maths
The Ghanaian currency is the cedi. Use currency converters on the Internet to discover what 100 cedi are worth in your currency. Calculate the value of 10 cedi and 20 cedi.

Citizenship
Kofi Annan is a Ghanaian statesman who led the United Nations as Secretary-General from 1997 to 2006. Discover the history and aims of the United Nations.

Design and Technology
Ghana produces cacao for use in chocolate production. Invent a new type of chocolate bar and design its packaging and plan an advertising campaign. You will need to think of a name, what special ingredients it contains, who will want to buy it – and how you will encourage them to try your new bar.

English
Write and decorate a brochure that is designed to encourage tourists to come and visit Ghana. Your brochure should include descriptions of Ghana's culture, wildlife and natural beauty.

Further information and index

Further reading

Facts At Your Fingertips: Africa, Derek Hall (Wayland 2008)
Festivals and Food: West Africa, Alison Brownlie Bojang (Wayland 2006)
Traditional Stories from West Africa, Robert Hull (Wayland 2006)

Web

http://ghana-net.com
This fun site has lots of useful information and video clips about Ghanaian life and culture.
www.ghanaweb.com
A huge site, which is an excellent source of information about the country, its people and their attitudes.
http://www.touringghana.com
The official website of Ghana Tourism, with information about the country's regions, festivals, history and tourism.

Index